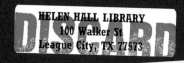

Apr 17

GLOW

Animals with Their Own Night-Lights

W. H. Beck

HOUGHTON MIFFLIN HARCOURT
Boston New York

For my science-loving parents, David and Barbara Hogue

Special thanks to the scientists Edith Widder and Steve Haddock for ensuring the
accuracy of this book, as well as editor Kate O'Sullivan, designer Cara Llewellyn,
and the rest of the team at Houghton Mifflin Harcourt.

Photo credits: p. 1: Alexander Semenov; pp. 3 and 24: Rob Sherlock; p. 4: Dale Darwin; pp. 5,
12/13, 15, and 25: Edith Widder; p. 6/7: Steve Axford; p. 8/9: Yume; p. 10: Peter David / Natural
Visions; pp. 11 and 20: David Shale; p. 14: David Wrobel; p. 16: Jessica Rozenkrantz; pp. 17 and
22: Steve Haddock; p. 18/19: photonewzealand; p. 21: Larry Madin © Woods Hole Oceanographic
Institution; p. 23: K. J. Osborn; p. 26/27: Paul Zahl; p. 28/29: Richard Smith; p. 30: Eric Röttinger.

Library of Congress Cataloging-in-Publication Data is on file.
ISBN 978-0-544-41666-6

Manufactured in USA
PHX 10 9 8 7 6 5 4 3 2
4500579064

FRONT JACKET PHOTO: The female humpback angler waves her light back
and forth like a fishing rod for smaller fish to come closer and investigate.
Meanwhile, she keeps her body still and her mouth open and ready.

TITLE PAGE PHOTO: The crystal jellyfish is normally almost see-through. But
when something bothers it, more than a hundred light-producing organs
glow green on the rim of its bell.

OPPOSITE: The cockatoo squid is also called the glass squid. Most of its body
is transparent, or clear, like glass, making it hard to see in the water. It even
uses lights under its eyes so that the non-transparent part of its body doesn't
leave a shadow.

It's called
bioluminescence
(by-oh-loo-mih-neh-sense).
Bioluminescence
is when living things make
their own light.

They glow.

You might know some animals that glow.

You might recognize fireflies, which aren't flies at all, but a type of beetle. Scientists think that their lights may warn predators, such as bats, that they aren't a good meal.

But others might be new to you.

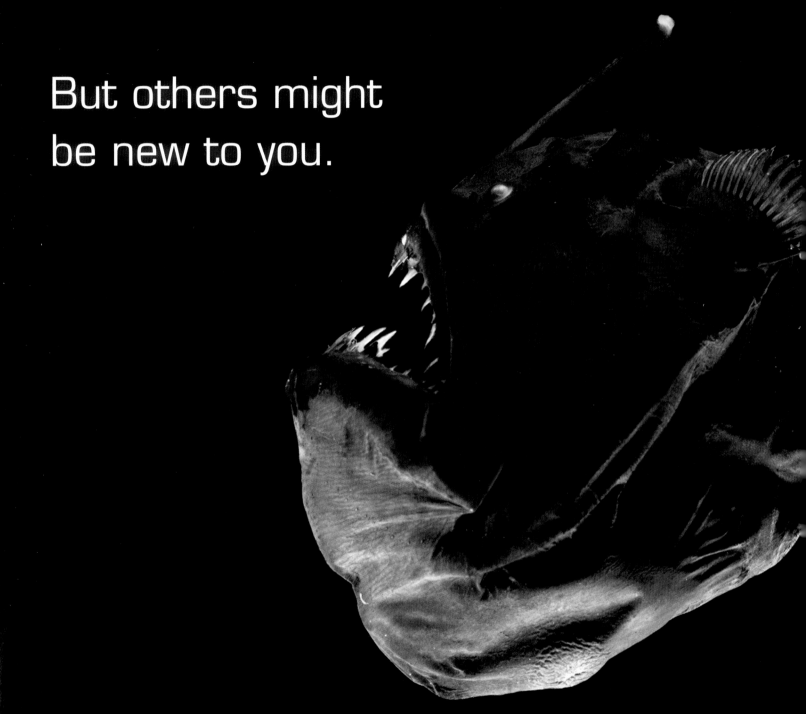

Anglerfish lure other fish to them with a glowing light organ.

Some glow on land.

Many fungi, such as these foxfire mushrooms growing on rotting wood, light up the forest floor.

Some glow in the air.

Fireflies blink and flash to "talk" to other fireflies.
They find their mate using their light, too.

But more than anywhere else on our planet, animals glow in the water. That's because sunlight can't reach very far under the waves. It's dark. So the animals make their own light.

They glow.

Water covers two-thirds of the earth. An estimated fifty to eighty percent of all life forms (including the white anglerfish and glowing sucker octopus seen here) are found under the ocean's surface.

Are you wondering *how* animals glow? They have special chemicals called luciferin (loo-sih-fer-in) and luciferase (loo-sih-fer-ase) in or on their bodies. These chemicals mix with oxygen and make light.

Why do they glow? Well . . .

They glow to hunt.

The scaly dragonfish lures its prey with a light near its
mouth. When a fish comes by to check it out, the dragonfish
opens its jaws and scoops it in!

They glow to hide.

Many ocean creatures, such as the jewel squid, use counter-illumination. They can adjust their lights so that their undersides match the sunlight above the water. Then the fish hunting them from below can't see them.

They glow to
find a friend.

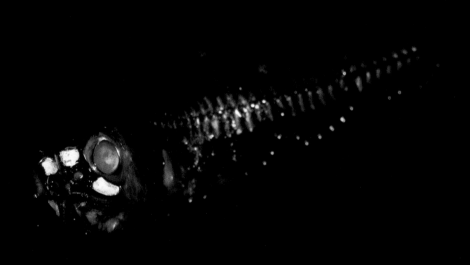

Not only is it dark deep in the ocean, but there's a lot of room. Lanternfish find other lanternfish with the lights on their sides. Bioluminescence is the most widely used form of communication on the planet.

They glow to lose an enemy.

A brittle star can drop an arm when it is in danger. Its enemy will follow the glowing arm, which allows the rest of the star to get away.

They glow
to trick.

Small fish follow the light on the tip of the gulper eel's tail, thinking it's a piece of food. They get close, then ... *gulp.* The gulper eel's hinged, pelican-like mouth allows it to swallow animals even bigger than it is.

They glow to invite.

Glowworms, like these in a cave in New Zealand, are actually firefly larvae. Their light draws insects into the cave. Then the glowworms snag them with sticky silk threads hung from the ceiling.

They glow to call for help.

Atolla jellyfish act as a burglar alarm. They light
up when attacked in the hope that a larger animal
will come eat their predator.

They glow to fight back.

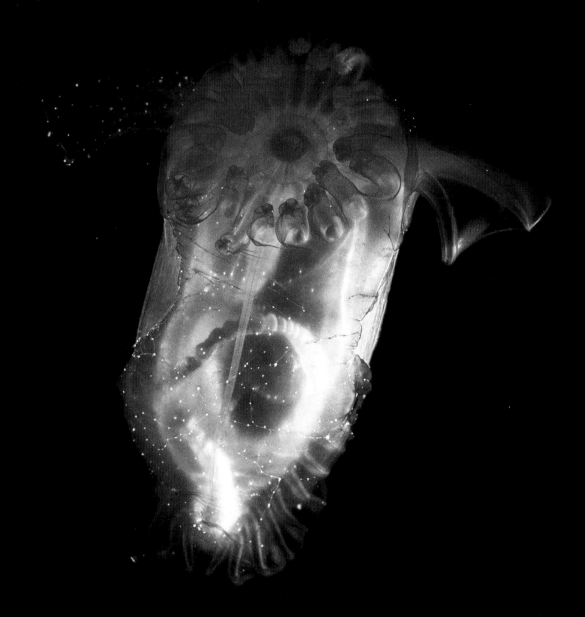

When the deep-sea Spanish dancer is threatened, its outer skin lights up, comes off, and sticks to its attacker. Now the predator is at risk of being spotted—and eaten—by its enemies. Meanwhile, the deep-sea dancer makes its getaway.

They glow to daze . . .

When threatened, the vampire squid spurts a cloud of
glowing ink at its predator, while it swims away.

. . . and dazzle.

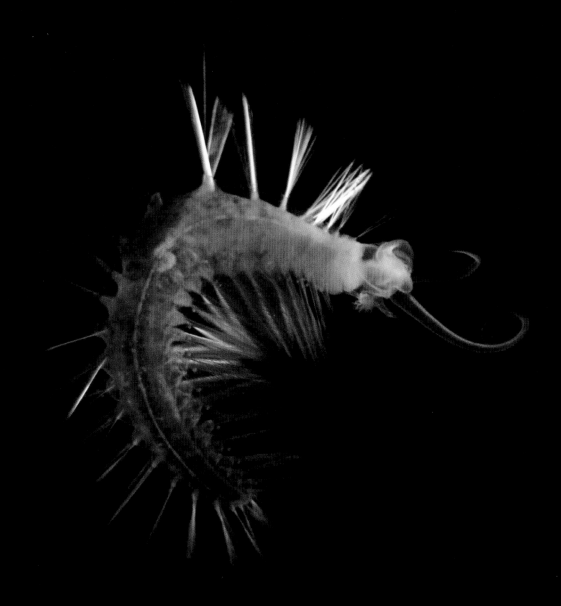

"Green bomber" worms release glowing
round balls when pursued.

And some glow for fun. (Well, not exactly. Scientists just don't know yet why some animals are bioluminescent.)

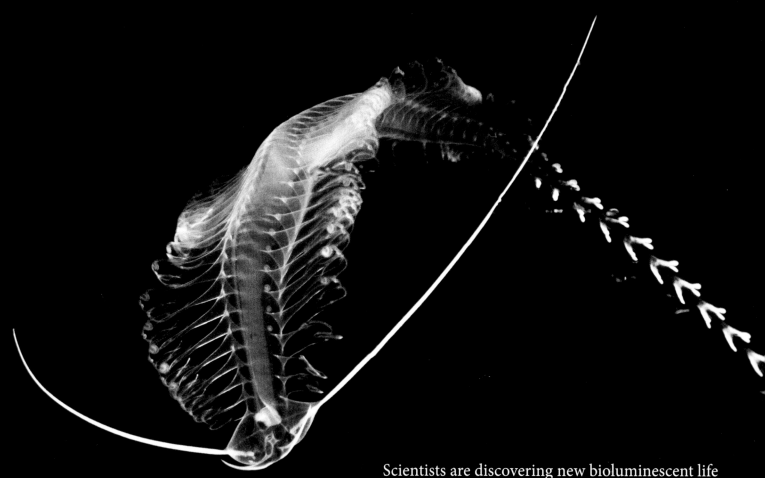

Scientists are discovering new bioluminescent life forms every day. But most of the reasons they glow are still mysteries. For example, no one knows why some tomopteris worms squeeze out yellow light that's invisible to almost all other sea creatures.

Large animals glow.

Siphonophores, such as the well-known Portugese man-of-war or this *Nanomia cara*, are stringy, jelly-like animals that drift through the water, snagging their prey with their tentacles. Some can be very long—the *Praya dubia* can stretch longer than a basketball court!

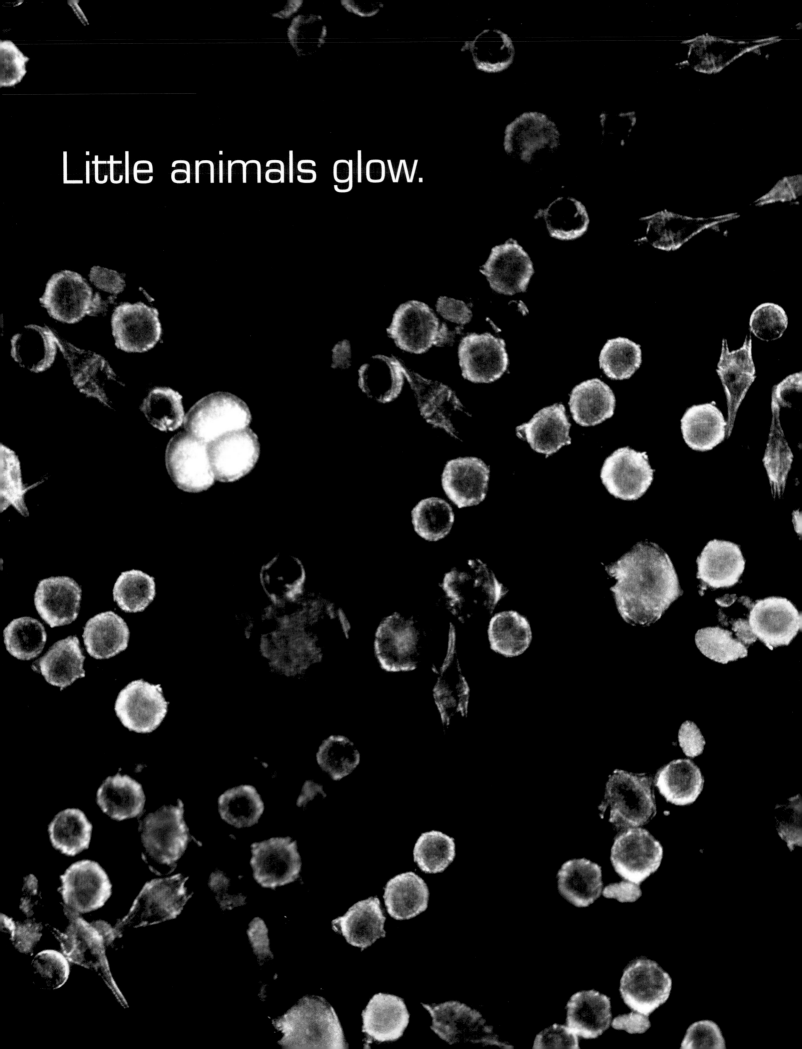

Little animals glow.

But if you have enough of them . . .

Some dinoflagellates (di-noh-flah-jel-ates; tiny one-celled animals that float in the ocean) light up when the small copepods and shrimp that eat them swim through their water. Their glow spotlights the copepods and shrimp so that larger fish eat them—and the dinoflagellates stay safe.

. . . they can have a BIG effect.

Sometimes bioluminescent dinoflagellates gather together and then get trapped in ocean bays, making the shoreline light up at night with each wave.

Some
living things
make their own
light.
They glow.
It's called
bioluminescence.
And now
you know.

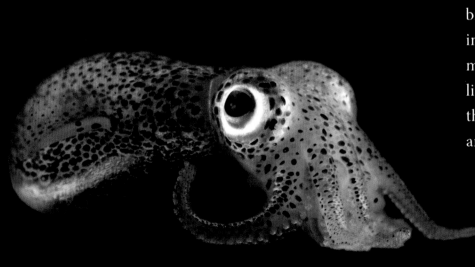

Hawaiian bobtail squid attract bioluminescent bacteria that live inside them. The bacteria then matches the color of the moonlight through the water, making the squid almost invisible to the animals they hunt.

While there is no doubt that the life forms in this book display amazing features and behavior, many of them are actually quite tiny—the size of an apple, or smaller! The photographs are enlarged so we can see the creatures' details.

Furthermore, these photographs are terribly hard to take and are quite rare. They are snapped deep underwater in total darkness with a flash. Sometimes that means the photographs are less clear than what we are used to seeing. Additionally, sometimes they do not capture the life form's bioluminescent aspects.

To help explain some of this, the drawings below highlight where the bioluminescence occurs, and also detail the true size of the organism and where they are found in nature.

black-devil anglerfish
(*Melanocetus johnsonii*)
Males, 1 inch (2.54 cm), females,
7 inches (17.78 cm); 3,200–13,000
feet deep (975–3,962 meters)

black-devil anglerfish
(*Melanocetus johnsonii*)
Males, 1 inch (2.54 cm), females,
7 inches (17.78 cm); 3,200–13,000
feet deep (975–3,962 meters)

scaly dragonfish
(*Stomias boa*)
8 inches (20.32 cm); 650–4,900
feet deep (198–1,494 meters)

gulper eel
(*Saccopharynx*)
6 feet (1.83 meters);
6,500–9,800 feet deep
(1,981–2,987 meters)

crystal jellyfish
(*Aequorea victoria*)
3 inches (7.62 cm); 18–20 feet
deep (5.5–6.1 meters)

foxfire mushrooms
(*Panellus stipticus*)
1 inch (2.54 cm) wide; forests of
Europe, Asia, and eastern North
America

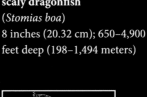

jewel squid
(*Histioteuthis*)
6 inches (15.24 cm); day, 1,300–
3,900 feet (396–1,189 meters),
night, 0–1,200 feet (0–366 meters)

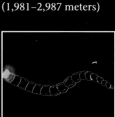

glowworm
(*Arachnocampa luminosa*)
.5–1.1 inches (1.2–2.9 cm); caves
in New Zealand

cockatoo squid
(*Galiteuthis phyllura*)
6 inches (15.2 cm), but can grow up
to 8 feet (2.44 meters); 980–4,500 feet
deep (299–1372 meters)

deep-sea white anglerfish
(*Haplophryne mollis*)
Males, .5 inches (1.27 cm), females,
2 inches (5.08 cm); 3,200–13,000 feet
deep (975–3,962 meters)

lanternfish
(*Diaphus*)
2–3 inches (5.08–7.62 cm);
270–3,000 feet deep
(82–914 meters)

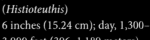

atolla jellyfish
(*Atolla wvyillei*)
1.4–1.6 inches (3.5–4.0 cm);
1,900–16,000 feet deep
(579–4,877 meters)

firefly
(*Photinus pyralis*)
.4 inches (1–1.4 cm); United
States, east of the Rocky
Mountains

glowing sucker octopus
(*Stauroteuthis syrtensis*)
Up to 12.5 inches (31.75 cm);
2,200–8,200 feet deep
(671–2,499 meters)

brittle star
(*Ophiura*)
Approximately 6 inches (15 cm);
2,700 feet deep (823 meters)

deep-sea Spanish dancer
(*Enypniastes eximia*)
Up to 9 inches (22.86 cm);
1,600–16,000 feet deep
(488–4,877 meters)

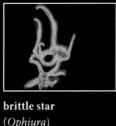

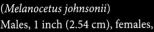

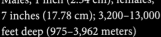

vampire squid
(*Vampyroteuthis infernalis*)
10 inches (25.4 cm);
2,100–4,900 feet deep
(640–1,494 meters)

tomopteris worm
(*Tomopteris helgolandica*)
1.6 inches long (4.06 cm);
0–13,000 feet deep
(0–4,000 meters)

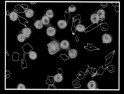

dinoflagellates
(*Dinoflagellates*)
.0002 –.08 inches
(5–2,000 micrometers);
on the surface of the ocean

green bomber worm
(*Swima bombiviridis*)
.6 inches (1.5 cm);
6,200–9,800 feet deep
(1,890–2,987 meters)

siphonophore
(*Nanomia cara*)
6.5 feet (2 meters), though the
siphonophore *Praya dubia* can
reach a length of 120–150 feet
(36.6– 45.7 meters); 1,300–7,200
feet deep (396–2,195 meters)

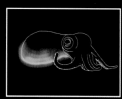

Hawaiian bobtail squid
(*Euprymna scolopes*)
1.4 inches (3.56 cm);
.8–1.6 inches deep
(2–4 cm)

Bibliography

American Museum of Natural History. Online information about the *Creatures of Light* exhibition. (www.amnh.org/exhibitions/past-exhibitions/creatures-of-light; accessed September 29, 2014.)

Barkan, Joanne. *Creatures That Glow.* New York: Doubleday Books for Young Readers, 1991.

Batten, Mary. *The Winking Blinking Sea: All About Bioluminescence.* Minneapolis: Millbrook Press, 2000.

BBC Nature. "Bioluminescence." (www.bbc.co.uk/nature/adaptations/Bioluminescence; accessed September 29, 2014.)

Berger, Melvin. *Creatures That Glow: A Book About Bioluminescent Animals.* New York: Scholastic, 1996.

Ganeri, Anita. *Creatures That Glow.* New York: Harry N. Abrams, 1995.

McClintock, Jack. "Splendor in the Dark." *Discover.* May 2004, pp. 50–57.

McKee, David A. *Fire in the Sea: Bioluminescence and Henry Compton's Art of the Deep.* College Station: Texas A&M University Press, 2014.

National Geographic. Education: "Bioluminescence." (education.nationalgeographic.com/education/encyclopedia/bioluminescence/?ar_a=1; accessed September 29, 2014.)

Nouvian, Claire. *The Deep: The Extraordinary Creatures of the Abyss.* Chicago: University of Chicago Press, 2007.

San Diego Natural History Museum. "Lights Alive." (www.sdnhm.org/archive/kids/lightsalive; accessed September 29, 2014.)

Sitarski, Anita. *Cold Light: Creatures, Discoveries, and Inventions That Glow.* Honesdale, PA: Boyds Mills Press, 2007.

Smithsonian National Museum of Natural History. *Ocean Portal: Find Your Blue:* "Bioluminescence." (ocean.si.edu/bioluminescence; accessed September 29, 2014.)

Tucker, Abigail. "Light Fantastic." *Smithsonian.* March 2013. pp. 50–59.

Wilson, Thérèse, and J. Woodland Hastings. *Bioluminescence: Living Lights, Lights for Living.* Cambridge: Harvard University Press, 2013.